FOREST PARK PUBLIC LIBRARY

3 2026 00607 9161

S0-AFM-981

JAN – – 2018

553.82   19.68
HAR

Harrison, Lorraine
Dazzling diamonds

Forest Park Public Library

The Glittering World of Gems

DAZZLING DIAMONDS

By Lorraine Harrison

FOREST PARK PUBLIC LIBRARY

JAN - - 2019

FOREST PARK, IL

Published in 2018 by
KidHaven Publishing, an Imprint of Greenhaven Publishing, LLC
353 3rd Avenue
Suite 255
New York, NY 10010

Copyright © 2018 KidHaven Publishing, an Imprint of Greenhaven Publishing, LLC.

All rights reserved. No part of this book may be reproduced in any form without permission in writing from the publisher, except by a reviewer.

Designer: Seth Hughes
Editor: Vanessa Oswald

Photo credits: Cover (left) chris kolaczan/Shutterstock.com; cover (right) Igor Masin/Shutterstock.com; cover, pp. 1–2, 4, 6, 8, 10, 12, 14, 16, 18, 20–21, back cover ILeysen/Shutterstock.com; p. 5 (inset) boykung/Shutterstock.com; p. 5 (main) Imfoto/Shutterstock.com; p. 7 zebra0209/Shutterstock.com; p. 9 Peter Johnson/Corbis/VCG/Getty Images; p. 11 Per-Anders Pettersson/Getty Images; p. 13 Alice Nerr/Shutterstock.com; p. 14 (inset), 21 (inset, middle) Hekerui/Wikimedia Commons; p. 15 (diamond) Roy Palmer/Shutterstock.com; p. 15 (main) Nejron Photo/Shutterstock.com; p. 17 (inset) everything possible/Shutterstock.com; p. 17 (main) wideweb/Shutterstock.com; p. 19 © iStockphoto.com/BanksPhotos; p. 20 (inset) JTB Photo/Contributor/Universal Images Group/Getty Images; p. 21 (inset, top) Chris 73/Wikimedia Commons; p. 21 (inset, bottom) Mark Perlstein/The LIFE Images Collection/Getty Images.

Cataloging-in-Publication Data

Names: Harrison, Lorraine.
Title: Dazzling diamonds / Lorraine Harrison.
Description: New York : KidHaven Publishing, 2018. | Series: The glittering world of gems | Includes index.
Identifiers: ISBN 9781534523098 (pbk.) | 9781534523050 (library bound) | ISBN 9781534522954 (6 pack) | ISBN 9781534523043 (ebook)
Subjects: LCSH: Diamonds–Juvenile literature. | Menralogy–Juvenile literature.
Classification: LCC QE393.H37 2018 | DDC 553.8'2–dc23

Printed in the United States of America

CPSIA compliance information: Batch #BS17KL: For further information contact Greenhaven Publishing LLC, New York, New York at 1-844-317-7404.

Please visit our website, www.greenhavenpublishing.com. For a free color catalog of all our high-quality books, call toll free 1-844-317-7404 or fax 1-844-317-7405.

CONTENTS

FROM THE EARTH TO THE JEWELRY STORE

Diamonds are found in beautiful necklaces and rings, but where do they come from before that? These shiny gemstones form deep inside the earth. Diamonds are a crystal form of the element carbon, which is one of Earth's most common elements. However, only a small amount of carbon forms diamonds.

Diamonds form when carbon is under high heat and **pressure** for a long time. It takes billions of years for diamonds to form in the earth!

Mining for Facts!

Diamonds move closer to Earth's surface after a **volcano** erupts, or explodes.

It takes a lot of work to make a diamond that comes from the earth look like the shiny diamonds seen in **jewelry** stores.

DIAMONDS IN AFRICA

Diamonds of the highest gem **quality** are generally found in central and southern Africa. Years ago, volcanoes sent these diamond crystals up near the surface. Once they got closer to the surface, these crystals blended with a soft blue rock called kimberlite.

In 1870, once the news spread of diamonds being found near Kimberley in South Africa, miners jumped at their chance to gather them. Diamond mining in this area lasted for 43 years, with miners finding about 6,000 pounds (2,722 kg) of diamonds. An empty mine called the Big Hole exists where the diamonds were found, and it's 702 feet (214 m) deep!

Mining for Facts!

Diamonds are also found in places such as Russia, India, Brazil, Siberia, China, and the United States.

Africa isn't the only place on Earth where diamonds are found. This diamond mine is in Russia.

DIFFERENT KINDS OF DIAMONDS

All raw diamonds start out as **transparent**, eight-sided crystals, which are cut and **polished**. Once this is done, they shine when light hits them. This makes them perfect for jewelry.

Most diamonds are colorless. Some come in different colors such as blue, green, red, yellow, or purple. These rare diamonds are called "fancy" diamonds. The colored diamonds form by other elements mixing with carbon, such as boron, which makes blue diamonds. Red diamonds are the most rare.

Mining for Facts!

Diamonds became the popular choice for rings starting in the late 1940s.

Colored diamonds such as these are very rare.

DIGGING FOR GEMS

Diamonds are brought to the earth's surface in the form of liquid rock. Once the liquid rock reaches the surface, it cools, hardens, and forms kimberlite. Whenever miners come across a kimberlite **deposit**, they dig into the earth and follow its path down. The miners hope to find diamonds at the end!

Miners use big machines and drills to remove diamonds from the earth. Sometimes these tools dig up a bunch of rocks and dirt the size of a house, only to find a few diamonds. It takes a lot of miners to operate these machines and find the diamonds.

These miners are searching for diamonds in the Wesselton Mine in South Africa.

MINING METHODS

Many diamond miners find gems using open-pit mining. The miners start by digging a hole straight down into a kimberlite deposit. Kimberlite mines are wide at the top but narrow at the bottom. The wide, bowl-shaped hole at the top is why they're called open-pit mines.

The miners use big machines to dig into the kimberlite rock in the mine. These machines break up the rock into smaller pieces. The miners keep following what's called a kimberlite pipe until they can't find any more diamonds. When miners find an area with a lot of diamonds, they also may dig narrow tunnels called shafts straight down into the kimberlite.

12

Mining for Facts!

After the rocks are collected from the mines, they are put on trucks to be sorted.

Two mining trucks are shown here taking loads of rocks away from an open-pit mine.

SHAPING DIAMONDS

Before cutting and polishing a diamond, a jeweler called a lapidary studies the gem. The jeweler picks out flaws to cut away from the diamond to make it stronger.

The lapidary decides what shape a diamond should be. These shapes include circle, oval, square, rectangle, pear, and heart. The gem is then cut into the shape using a diamond-tipped saw and a lot of water. Jewelers need to be careful when shaping diamonds. Although diamonds are very hard, they're also **brittle** and can easily crack if too much pressure is forced on them.

Mining for Facts!

Some say the Hope Diamond is cursed because its former owner had bad luck while owning it.

14

Shaping diamonds requires the jeweler to have a good eye and a steady hand.

ADDING FACETS

Facets are **grinded** onto diamonds after a lapidary has cut them into a basic shape. These facets are flat sides that allow the diamond to shine in light.

Lapidaries use a faceting machine to place the facets onto the diamonds. Since diamonds are harder than other gems, it can be tough to figure out where to put the facets. Lapidaries are trained for a long time before they can add facets to a diamond.

Faceted diamonds have been made for centuries. The first faceted diamonds were made in 1375 in Nuremberg, Germany.

Mining for Facts!
A round-shaped diamond generally has 57 to 58 facets.

A lapidary is shown here looking at a diamond before putting the finishing facets onto it.

A DIAMOND'S VALUE

Every diamond has different features, which help decide its value. Each diamond is priced by its color, **clarity**, cut, and **carat** weight. Colorless diamonds are more valued than cloudy or slightly yellow diamonds. However, naturally colored diamonds are very rare and valuable. A diamond with flaws reduces its clarity and can make it less valuable.

The one feature the jeweler has control of is the diamond's cut. This makes the diamond more or less valuable depending on how well the jeweler has been trained to cut a diamond.

Mining for Facts!

The United States buys more diamonds than any other country.

A jeweler is shown here putting a cut diamond into a ring.

DIAMONDS USED TO MAKE DIAMONDS

The only thing that can scratch a diamond is another diamond. Because of this, 80 percent of the diamonds mined every year are used to make cutting, grinding, and polishing tools. These tools are used to cut and shape diamonds and other gems.

Mining for Facts!

Shown here is a diamond blade, which is a saw blade that has diamonds pressed into the edges. It's used for cutting hard materials, such as stone, concrete, glass, and diamonds.

RARE DIAMOND FINDS

What: The Cullinan Diamond is the largest gem-quality rough diamond ever found. It was cut into several gems, including the Great Star of Africa, shown here, and Second Star of Africa.

When: 1905

Where: the Premier Mine in South Africa

Weight: Before it was cut into pieces, the diamond weighed more than 3,106 carats (621.2 g).

Value: about $400 million

What: The Hope Diamond is a blue-colored diamond. It has been on display at the Smithsonian Museum since 1958.

When: 1642

Where: India

Weight: Originally, the diamond weighed 112 carats (22.4 g), but after being cut, weighs just over 45 carats (9 g).

Value: about $350 million

What: The Uncle Sam Diamond is the largest diamond ever found in the United States.

When: 1924

Where: the Crater of Diamonds State Park in Arkansas, which is the world's only diamond mine open to the public

Weight: Originally, the diamond weighed more than 40 carats (8 g) and was later cut down to 12.4 carats (2.5 g).

Value: Sidney de Young, who purchased it in 1971, sold it to an anonymous private collector for $150,000.

21

GLOSSARY

brittle: Likely to break or crack.

carat: A unit used to weigh diamonds. One carat is equal to 200 milligrams, or 0.007 ounce.

clarity: The state of being clear.

deposit: An amount of a mineral in the ground that built up over a period of time.

grind: To shape or smooth something with a rough surface.

jewelry: Pieces of metal, often holding gems, that are worn on the body.

polish: To make something smooth and shiny by rubbing it with a soft cloth.

pressure: A force that pushes on something else.

quality: The standard or grade of something.

transparent: Letting light shine through.

volcano: An opening in a planet's surface through which hot, liquid rock sometimes flows.

FOR MORE INFORMATION

Websites

Gem Kids: Diamonds
gemkids.gia.edu/gem/diamond
This website includes colorful illustrations and fun facts about diamonds.

National Geographic Kids: Diamond
kids.nationalgeographic.com/explore/science/diamond/#diamonds-raw.jpg
This website provides cool pictures and interesting information about diamonds.

Books

Farndon, John. *Rocks, Minerals and Gems*. Richmond Hill, ON: Firefly Books, 2016.

Green, Dan. *The Rock and Gem Book: A Visual Encyclopedia of the Earth's Treasures*. New York, NY: DK Publishing, 2016.

Publisher's note to educators and parents: Our editors have carefully reviewed these websites to ensure that they are suitable for students. Many websites change frequently, however, and we cannot guarantee that a site's future contents will continue to meet our high standards of quality and educational value. Be advised that students should be closely supervised whenever they access the Internet.

INDEX